# Cool French Cooking

## Fun and Tasty Recipes for Kids

Lisa Wagner

## TO ADULT HELPERS

You're invited to assist up-and-coming chefs! As children learn to cook, they develop new skills, gain confidence, and make some delicious food. What's more, it's a lot of fun!

Efforts have been made to keep the recipes in this book authentic yet simple. You will notice that some of the recipes are more difficult than others. Be there to help children with these recipes, but encourage them to do as much as they can on their own. Also encourage them to try new foods and experiment with their own ideas. Building creativity into the cooking process encourages children to think like real chefs.

Before getting started, set some ground rules about using the kitchen, cooking tools, and ingredients. Most importantly, adult supervision is a must whenever a child uses the stove, oven, or sharp tools.

So, put on your aprons and stand by. Let your young chefs take the lead. Watch and learn. Taste their creations. Praise their efforts. Enjoy the culinary adventure!

## visit us at www.abdopublishing.com

Published by ABDO Publishing Company, a division of ABDO, P.O. Box 398166, Minneapolis, Minnesota 55439. Copyright © 2011 by Abdo Consulting Group, Inc. International copyrights reserved in all countries. No part of this book may be reproduced in any form without written permission from the publisher. Checkerboard Library™ is a trademark and logo of ABDO Publishing Company.

Printed in the United States of America, North Mankato, Minnesota
102010
012011

 PRINTED ON RECYCLED PAPER

Design and Production: Colleen Dolphin, Mighty Media, Inc.
Art Direction: Colleen Dolphin
Series Editor: Liz Salzmann
Food Production: Frankie Tuminelly
Photo Credits: Colleen Dolphin, iStockphoto (Steve Debenport, Rainbowphoto), Photodisc, Shutterstock

The following manufacturers/names appearing in this book are trademarks: Gold Medal®, Heinz®, Market Pantry®, Morton®, Pyrex®, Roundy's®, Swanson®, Target®

Library of Congress Cataloging-in-Publication Data

Wagner, Lisa, 1958-
  Cool French cooking : fun and tasty recipes for kids / Lisa Wagner.
    p. cm. -- (Cool world cooking)
  Includes index.
  ISBN 978-1-61714-660-2
  1. Cooking, French--Juvenile literature. I. Title.
  TX719.W25 2011
  641.5944--dc22
                                    2010022192

# Table of Contents

# Explore the Foods of France!

French cooking is famous. Many of the world's greatest chefs trained in France. French cooking is an art and has been for centuries. Long ago, chefs who cooked for kings and queens wanted to be noticed. They worked hard to invent new dishes!

Today, the French are still serious about food. It can take hours to eat lunch! Most people shop for food every day in outdoor markets. Fresh food is one of the secrets to French cooking!

France has mountains, forests, valleys, and a coastline. These different areas offer a variety of **delicious** foods. Goats, cows, and sheep graze in the mountains. Mushrooms grow in the forest. Seafood and fish come from the coasts. Fruits, vegetables, olives, and herbs grow well in valleys too. Are you ready for a tasty French adventure? Put on your aprons and off we go!

## GET THE PICTURE!

When a step number in a recipe has a dotted circle around it, look for the picture that goes with it. The circle around the photo will be the same color as the step number.

4 →

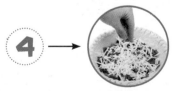

## HOW DO YOU SAY THAT?

You may come across some French words you've never heard of in this book. Don't worry! There's a pronunciation guide on page 30!

# The Basics

Get going in the right direction
with a few important basics!

## ASK PERMISSION

Before you cook, get permission to use the kitchen, cooking tools, and ingredients. When you need help, ask. Always get help when you use the stove or oven.

## GET ORGANIZED

- Being well organized is a chef's secret ingredient for success!

- Read through the entire recipe before you do anything else.

- Gather all your cooking tools and ingredients.

- Get the ingredients ready. The list of ingredients tells how to prepare each item.

- Put each prepared ingredient into a separate bowl.

- Read the recipe instructions carefully. Do the steps in the order they are listed.

## GOOD COOKING TAKES PREP WORK

Many ingredients need preparation before they are used. Look at a recipe's ingredients list. Some ingredients will have words such as chopped, sliced, or grated next to them. These words tell you how to prepare the ingredients.

Give yourself plenty of time and be patient. Always wash fruits and vegetables. Rinse them well and pat them dry with a **towel**. Then they won't slip when you cut them. After you prepare each ingredient, put it in a separate prep bowl. Now you're ready!

## BE SMART, BE SAFE

- If you use the stove or oven, you need an adult with you.
- Never use the stove or oven if you are home alone.
- Always get an adult to help with the hot jobs, such as frying with oil.
- Have an adult nearby when you are using sharp tools such as knives, peelers, graters, or food processors.
- Always turn pot handles to the back of the stove. This helps prevent accidents and spills.
- Work slowly and carefully. If you get hurt, let an adult know right away!

## BE NEAT, BE CLEAN

- Start with clean hands, clean tools, and a clean work surface.
- Tie back long hair so it stays out of the way and out of the food.
- Roll up your sleeves.
- An apron will protect your clothes from spills and splashes.
- Chef hats are **optional**!

## KEY SYMBOLS

In this book, you will see some symbols beside the recipes. Here is what they mean.

**HOT STUFF!**
The recipe requires the use of a stove or oven. You need adult assistance and supervision.

**SUPER SHARP!**
A sharp tool such as a peeler, knife, or grater is needed. Get an adult to stand by.

**EVEN COOLER!**
This symbol means adventure! Give it a try! Get inspired and invent your own cool ideas.

## No Germs Allowed!

Raw eggs and raw meat have bacteria in them. These bacteria are killed when food is cooked. But they can survive out in the open and make you sick! After you handle raw eggs or meat, wash your hands, tools, and work surfaces with soap and water. Keep everything clean!

# The Tool Box

A box on the bottom of the first page of each recipe lists the tools you need.
When you come across a tool you don't know, turn back to these pages.

**SERRATED KNIFE**

**SMALL SHARP KNIFE**

**CUTTING BOARD**

**MEASURING CUPS**

**MEASURING SPOONS**

**LIQUID MEASURING CUP**

**PREP BOWLS**

**MIXING BOWLS**

**WOODEN SPOON**

**PASTRY BRUSH**

**TABLE KNIFE**

**FORK**

**PEELER**

**TONGS**

**GRATER**

**CAN OPENER**

**SPATULA**

**PAPER TOWELS**

**BAKING SHEET**

**SAUCEPAN**

**STRAINER**

**KITCHEN STRING**

**SMALL JAR WITH LID**

**POT HOLDERS**

**FRYING PAN**

**DINNER PLATE**

**ALUMINUM FOIL**

**ROUND GLASS BAKING DISH**

**9 × 9-INCH BAKING DISH**

**WHISK**

**SOUP POT**

**MEAT THERMOMETER**

**SOUP BOWL**

**TIMER**

9

# Cool Cooking Terms

Here are some basic cooking terms and the actions that go with them. Whenever you need a reminder, just turn back to these pages.

## FIRST THINGS FIRST

Always wash fruit and vegetables well. Rinse them under cold water. Pat them dry with a **towel**. Then they won't slip when you cut them.

### CHOP

*Chop* means to cut things into small pieces with a knife.

### GRATE

*Grate* means to shred something into small pieces using a grater.

### ARRANGE

*Arrange* means to place food in a certain order or pattern.

### MIX

*Mix* means to stir ingredients together, usually with a large spoon.

## WHISK

*Whisk* means to beat quickly by hand with a whisk or fork.

## SLICE

*Slice* means to cut food into pieces of the same thickness.

## MINCE

*Mince* means to cut the food into the tiniest possible pieces. Garlic is often minced.

## SAUTÉ

*Sauté* means to fry quickly in a pan using a small amount of oil or butter.

## PEEL

*Peel* means to remove the skin, often with a peeler.

## GREASE

*Grease* means to coat a surface with oil or butter so food doesn't stick.

# The Coolest Ingredients

**YELLOW POTATOES**

**RED POTATOES**

**WHITE ONION**

**SCALLIONS**

**PLUM TOMATOES**

**BLACKBERRIES**

**GARLIC**

**BLACK OLIVES**

**ROMAINE LETTUCE**

**GREEN BEANS**

**RASPBERRIES**

**FRESH PARSLEY**

**FRESH THYME**

**FRESH ROSEMARY**

**HERBS DE PROVENCE**

**FRESH OREGANO**

**GROUND PEPPER**

**FRESH DILL**

**KOSHER SALT**

**SALT**

# Allergy Alert!

Some people have a reaction when they eat certain foods. If you have any allergies, you know what it's all about. An allergic reaction can require emergency **medical** help. Nut allergies can be especially **dangerous**. Before you serve anything made with nuts or peanut oil, ask if anyone has a nut allergy.

# Herbs de Provence

Herbs de Provence is a special mixture of dried herbs. It includes thyme, savory, rosemary, marjoram, basil, oregano, and lavender. The mixture was invented in the Provence region of France. Herbs grow well in this sunny, southern region.

**ALL-PURPOSE FLOUR**

**BEEF BROTH**

**HALF & HALF**

**MILK**

**EGG**

**CANNED TUNA**

**SWISS CHEESE**

**GRUYÈRE CHEESE**

**PREPARED PIE SHELL**

**FRENCH BAGUETTE**

**BUTTER**

**BREAD**

**VANILLA EXTRACT**

**RED WINE VINEGAR**

**OLIVE OIL**

**SUGAR**

**POWDERED SUGAR**

**WHOLE CHICKEN**

**DELI HAM**

**BACON**

# Perfect Hardboiled Eggs!

Carefully set the eggs in a medium saucepan. Add cold water until it is one inch above the eggs. Bring the water to a boil, uncovered, over medium-high heat. Reduce the heat to medium and boil the eggs for 3 minutes.

Now cover the pan and turn off the heat. Let the eggs sit for 17 minutes. Then ask an adult to help you put the pan in the sink. Remove the cover. Run cold water over the eggs until they are cool.

Tap the large end of an egg on the counter to crack it. Remove the shell completely. Try holding the egg under running water while peeling it. This can make it easier!

# French Extras

Serve these with roast chicken or other main dishes!

## GREAT GREEN BEANS FROM PROVENCE

Makes 6 servings

### INGREDIENTS

2 tablespoons olive oil
1 small onion, finely chopped
2 cloves garlic, minced
1 teaspoon herbs de Provence (see page 13)
1 pound green beans, ends trimmed
2 plum tomatoes, chopped
salt
ground pepper

### TOOLS

• prep bowls
• measuring spoons
• cutting board
• small sharp knife
• serrated knife
• frying pan
• wooden spoon
• pot holders
• timer

1 Heat the oil in a frying pan over medium heat.

2 Add the onions. Sauté for 5 minutes, mixing with a wooden spoon.

3 Add the garlic and herbs de Provence. Sauté for 1 minute.

4 Add the beans. Sauté for 8 minutes.

5 Add the tomatoes. Mix gently for 3 minutes.

6 Add salt and pepper to taste.

# PERFECT POMMES ANNA

Makes 6 servings

### INGREDIENTS

6 yellow potatoes, peeled and sliced very thin
1 stick butter, melted
salt and ground pepper

### TOOLS

- peeler
- cutting board
- small sharp knife
- small saucepan
- pastry brush
- 9 x 9-inch glass baking dish
- aluminum foil
- pot holders
- timer

**1** Preheat the oven to 425 degrees.

**2** Melt the butter in a small saucepan over very low heat. Remove from heat.

**3** Brush a little butter on the bottom of the baking dish.

**4** Put a layer of potatoes in the pan. Brush the tops evenly with melted butter. Sprinkle lightly with salt and pepper.

**5** Continue to make layers of potatoes, butter, salt, and pepper.

**6** Put butter on one side of the aluminum foil. Put the foil butter side down over the pan. Press it onto the potatoes.

**7** Bake for 30 minutes.

**8** Remove the foil. Bake for 30 more minutes or until potatoes are tender.

**9** Remove from the oven. Run a knife around the edge of the pan.

# Superb Salad Niçoise

This amazing salad is a meal in itself!

MAKES 4 LARGE SALADS

## INGREDIENTS

½ pound fresh green beans, ends trimmed

4 small red potatoes

2 tablespoons red wine vinegar

5–6 tablespoons olive oil

¼ teaspoon salt

½ teaspoon ground pepper

2 tablespoons chopped fresh herbs (oregano, parsley, dill, thyme, or a combination)

1 head romaine lettuce, washed and dried

4 plum tomatoes, sliced

4 hard-boiled eggs, peeled and sliced (see page 15)

6-ounce can tuna, rinsed and drained in a strainer

20 black olives

**TOOLS:** saucepans with covers, measuring cup, measuring spoons, small sharp knife, serrated knife, cutting board, small jar with lid, paper towels, can opener, strainer, prep bowls, timer, 4 dinner plates

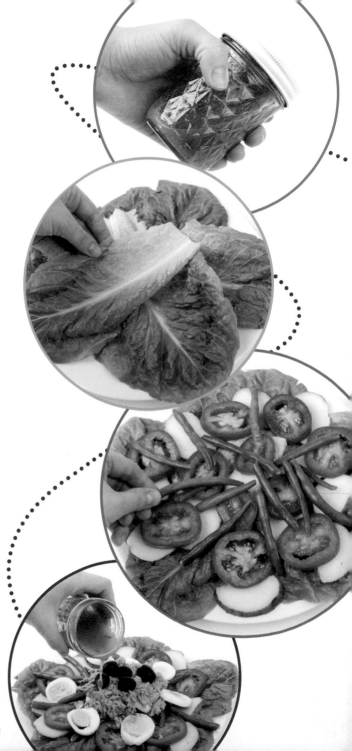

**1** Boil the beans in 3 cups of water for five minutes. Drain them in a strainer and rinse with cold water. Refrigerate the beans until you are ready to use them.

**2** Cover the potatoes with water in a medium saucepan. Bring to a boil, then reduce the heat to low. **Simmer** the potatoes for 15 minutes. Check the potatoes for doneness. A small sharp knife should go through the potato easily. If the potatoes are still too firm, continue simmering until the knife goes through easily.

**3** Use a strainer to drain the potatoes. Rinse with cold water. Chill for at least 1 hour in the refrigerator. Then cut them into slices.

**4** Put the vinegar, oil, salt, pepper, and herbs in a small jar with a tight-fitting lid. Shake until the ingredients are well blended. This is the dressing.

**5** Divide the lettuce evenly between four dinner plates. Spread the lettuce leaves around each plate.

**6** Arrange the potatoes, tomatoes, beans, eggs, tuna, and olives evenly over each plate of lettuce.

**7** Pour some of the dressing on each **salad** and serve.

# Fun French Onion Soup

*Several great flavors all in one pot!*

MAKES 4 BOWLS OF SOUP

## INGREDIENTS

8 ¾-inch thick slices of French baguette

2 tablespoons olive oil

4 large onions, sliced into thin rings

4 cups beef broth

1 cup grated Swiss cheese

salt

ground pepper

**TOOLS:**    prep bowls    grater    baking sheet    soup pot
cutting board    measuring spoons    timer    spatula
small sharp knife    measuring cups    wooden spoon    4 soup bowls

**1** Preheat the oven to 350 degrees.

**2** Put the slices of baguette on a baking sheet. Bake for 5 minutes. Flip the slices over and bake for 5 more minutes. Remove from oven and let cool.

**3** Heat the olive oil in a soup pot. Add the onions and cook over low heat for at least 30 minutes. Use a wooden spoon to mix the onions every few minutes. The onions are ready when they are deep golden brown.

**4** Add the broth to the pot. Bring to a boil over high heat. Cover the pot and turn the heat low. **Simmer** for 20 minutes.

**5** Divide the soup into four bowls. Put two slices of baked baguette in each bowl.

**6** Sprinkle ¼-cup grated cheese over each bowl of soup. Serve with salt and pepper.

### Even Cooler!

Add fresh herbs to this soup while it simmers. Use thyme, parsley, rosemary, or a combination of all three!

# Classic Croque Monsieur

## INGREDIENTS

4 slices of deli ham
½ cup grated Swiss cheese
4 slices bread
2 eggs
1 tablespoon half & half
2 tablespoons butter

A yummy French sandwich with a crunch!

MAKES 2 SANDWICHES

**TOOLS:** measuring cup  prep bowls  mixing bowl  frying pan  pot holders
measuring spoons  grater  whisk  spatula

1. Put two slices of ham and half of the cheese between two slices of bread. Put the remaining ham and cheese between the other two slices of bread.

2. Whisk together the eggs and half & half in a mixing bowl.

3. Dip each side of the sandwiches in the egg mixture.

4. Melt the butter in a frying pan. Fry the sandwiches over low heat until they are golden brown on the bottom.

5. Use a spatula to flip the sandwiches over. Cook until the other side is golden brown and the cheese is melted.

## Even Cooler!

Use herbed bread instead of plain white or wheat bread. Bread with rosemary or dill in it makes a **delicious** Croque Monsieur!

# Lovely Quiche Lorraine

A perfect meal for breakfast, lunch, or dinner!

MAKES 4 SERVINGS

## INGREDIENTS

1 unbaked, prepared pie shell

6 ounces sliced bacon

4 scallions, chopped

3 ounces Gruyére cheese (¾ cup grated)

4 eggs

1 cup half & half

¼ teaspoon ground pepper

**TOOLS:** baking sheet · prep bowls · measuring cups · measuring spoons · small sharp knife · cutting board · fork · grater · pot holders · timer · frying pan · tongs · spatula · paper towels · mixing bowl · whisk

**1** Preheat the oven. Follow the directions on the pie shell package.

**2** Poke holes in the bottom of the pie shell with a fork. Put the shell on a baking sheet. Bake the shell for half the time recommended on the package. Take the shell out of the oven. Set the oven to 350 degrees.

**3** Cook the bacon slices in a frying pan using medium heat. Use tongs to turn the bacon so it cooks evenly. When the bacon is lightly browned, remove it from the frying pan. Put it on paper **towels** to dry. Leave the bacon grease in the frying pan.

**4** Cook the scallions in the bacon grease for 2 minutes. Remove the scallions from the frying pan. Cut the bacon into ½-inch pieces. Put the bacon, scallions, and cheese in the pie shell.

**5** Whisk together the eggs, half & half, and pepper. Pour the egg mixture over the bacon and cheese. Bake for 30 to 35 minutes. Test for doneness by **inserting** a knife in the center. If the knife comes out clean the quiche is done. If there is batter sticking to the knife, bake for 5 more minutes. Let the quiche sit for 5 minutes. Cut into four pieces and serve.

## Even Cooler!

- Add ⅛ teaspoon ground nutmeg for an **authentic** French taste!

- Use 1 cup of chopped cooked ham instead of the bacon.

# Savory Roast Chicken

Simple to make and delicious to eat!

MAKES 4 TO 6 SERVINGS

### INGREDIENTS

1 whole chicken,
  between 3 and 4 pounds
**kosher** salt
ground pepper

**TOOLS:**  baking sheet  kitchen string  meat thermometer
measuring spoons  pot holders  sharp knife
paper towels  timer  cutting board

1. Preheat the oven to 450 degrees.

2. Rinse the chicken inside and out and use paper **towels** to dry it. Sprinkle 1 teaspoon **kosher** salt and ¼ teaspoon pepper inside the chicken.

3. Cross the ends of the legs. Tie them together with a piece of kitchen string.

4. Put the chicken in the baking sheet with the breast side up. Sprinkle 1 tablespoon kosher salt over the chicken.

5. Put the chicken in the oven for 1 hour. Ask an adult to use a meat **thermometer** to see if the chicken is done. **Insert** it between the leg and thigh but not touching a bone. When the thermometer reads 165 degrees the chicken is done.

6. Take the chicken out of the oven and let it sit for 15 minutes. Ask an adult to cut the chicken into pieces.

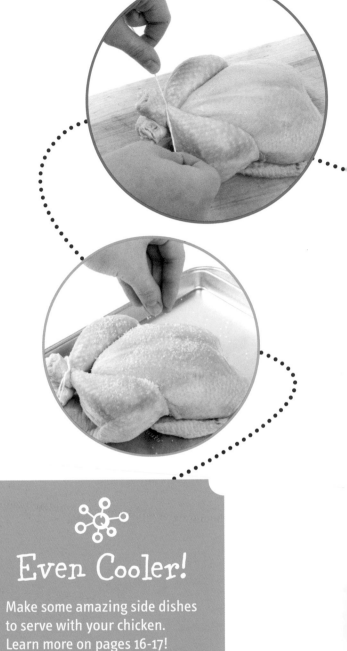

## Even Cooler!

Make some amazing side dishes to serve with your chicken. Learn more on pages 16-17!

# Very Berry Clafoutis

*A sweet and creamy fresh fruit dessert!*

MAKES 9 SERVINGS

## INGREDIENTS

butter

3 cups fresh raspberries
or blackberries

⅔ cup sugar

3 eggs

⅛ teaspoon salt

1 tablespoon vanilla extract

½ cup white flour

1 cup milk

½ cup powdered sugar

**TOOLS:** glass pie dish | measuring spoons | strainer | whisk | pot holders
paper towels | measuring cups | mixing bowl | table knife | timer

**1** Preheat the oven to 350 degrees. Grease the bottom and sides of the pie dish with butter.

**2** Wash the berries and set them on paper **towels**. Gently pat the berries dry. Arrange the berries evenly over the bottom of the buttered pie plate.

**3** In a mixing bowl, whisk together the sugar and eggs for 1 minute. Keep whisking while you add the salt, vanilla, and flour.

**4** Whisk in the milk. Pour the mixture evenly over the berries.

**5** Bake for 50 to 55 minutes until the clafoutis is puffy and brown. Test for doneness by **inserting** a knife in the center. When the knife comes out clean, the clafoutis is done. If there is a little batter sticking to the knife, bake for a few more minutes.

**6** Remove the pan from the oven. Put the powdered sugar in a strainer. Gently wave the strainer back and forth over the clafoutis. Cut into nine pieces. Serve warm.

## Even Cooler!

Use cherries instead of raspberries or blackberries. Wash the cherries and dry them gently with paper **towels**. Cut all the way around each cherry with a small sharp knife. Pry the halves apart and remove the pit.

# Wrap it Up!

Now you know how to make **delicious** French dishes! What did you learn? Did you try any new foods? Learning about recipes from around the world teaches you a lot. You learn about different **cultures**, climates, geography, and tastes.

Making international dishes also teaches you about new languages. Did you learn any new French words in this book? These new words will help you sound like a native speaker. You'll be able to use them at restaurants and **grocery stores**.

Clafoutis (klah-foo-TEE)

Croque Monsieur (croak miss-YOOR)

Herbs de Provence (airb deh pro-VAHNCE)

Niçoise (nee-SWAZZ)

Pommes Anna (pawmz AHH-nuh)

Provence (pro-VAHNCE)

Quiche Lorraine (KEESH luh-RANE)

# Glossary

**authentic** – real or true.

**culture** – the behavior, beliefs, art, and other products of a particular group of people.

**dangerous** – able or likely to cause harm or injury.

**delicious** – very pleasing to taste or smell.

**grocery store** – a place where you buy food items.

**insert** – to stick something into something else.

**kosher** – prepared according to Jewish law.

**medical** – having to do with doctors or the science of medicine.

**optional** – something you can choose, but is not required.

**salad** – a mixture of raw vegetables usually served with a dressing.

**simmer** – to stew gently at a soft boil.

**thermometer** – a tool used to measure temperature.

**towel** – a cloth or paper used for cleaning or drying.

# Web Sites

To learn more about cool cooking, visit ABDO Publishing Company on the World Wide Web at **www.abdopublishing. com.** Web sites about cool cooking are featured on our Book Links page. These links are routinely monitored and updated to provide the most current information available.

# Index